Especially for young readers

The Mini Page

How the U.S. Government Works

by
Betty Debnam

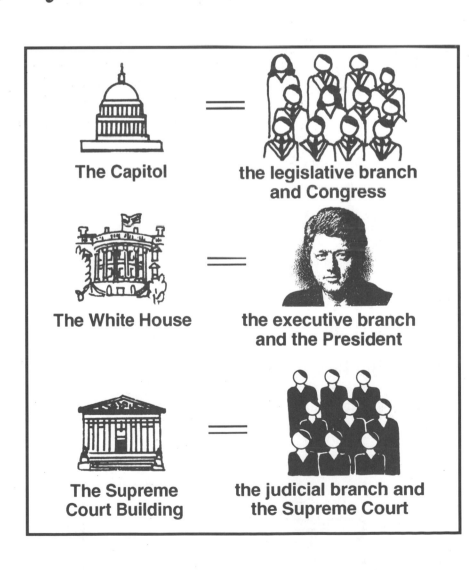

The Capitol = the legislative branch and Congress

The White House = the executive branch and the President

The Supreme Court Building = the judicial branch and the Supreme Court

Contents

Introduction

What Happens in Washington, D.C.? ... **3**

The Constitution

The Constitution **4-5**

Separation of Powers **6**

Checks and Balances **7**

The Lawmaking Branch

Article I of the Constitution **8**

The Busy Congressional Members **9**

Help for Members of Congress **10-11**

How a Bill Becomes a Law **12-13**

The Capitol **14-15**

The Executive Branch

Article II of the Constitution **16**

The President's Job **17**

The President's Many Hats **18-19**

The President's Cabinet **20-21**

The White House **22-23**

The Judicial Branch

Article III of the Constitution **24**

The Supreme Court **25**

The Justices at Work **26**

Chief Justices of the United States ... **27**

The Supreme Court Building **28-29**

Let's Visit the National Archives **30-31**

Newspaper Readers Learn About the U.S. Government **32**

What Happens in Washington, D.C.?

Washington, D.C., is our nation's capital. Do you know what happens there? This Mini Page book will take you to some of the city's most important buildings to show you who works there and what their jobs include.

The people who work in Washington, D.C., are very important, because many of them work for the federal, or national, government. They work together to help run our country. People have been doing this work for over 200 years.

We often use buildings to represent the branches of government and the people who work in them. Look for these symbols in the following pages:

The White House = **the executive branch and the President**

The Capitol = **the legislative branch and Congress**

The Supreme Court Building = **the judicial branch and the Supreme Court**

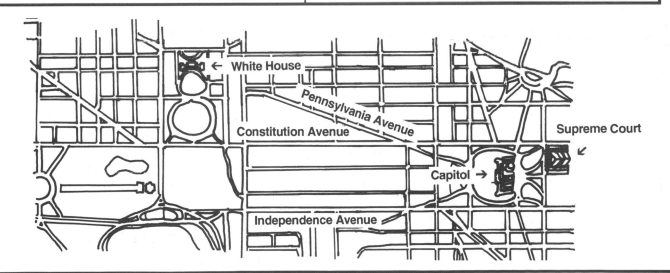

← White House
Pennsylvania Avenue
Constitution Avenue
Supreme Court ↙
Capitol →
Independence Avenue

Draw It

TO DO

Does your own hometown have certain buildings where people work to help run the government? Where are they? Work with a partner to draw and label a map of your town, showing these buildings. Make a list of what goes on in each one.

The Constitution

The Constitution is the main plan for governing our country. It is probably the single most important document we have as a nation. The writers who created it in 1787 made sure that every part was worded very carefully.

As President of the Constitutional Convention, George Washington was the first to sign the Constitution.

The Preamble

We the People of the United States, in order to form a more perfect union, establish justice, insure domestic tranquility, provide for the common defense, promote the general welfare, and secure the blessings of liberty to ourselves and our posterity, do ordain and establish this Constitution for the United States of America.

The original Constitution covered these subjects:

Article I:
The Congress.

Article II:
The President.

Article III:
The judges and national courts.

Article IV:
How states relate to each other and to the national government.

Article V:
How the Constitution can be amended or changed.

Article VI:
The Constitution as the supreme law of the land.

Article VII:
Ratification or approval.

Amendments to the Constitution

The first 10 amendments are called the Bill of Rights. These basic rights were added in 1791.

1st:

 Freedom of religion.

 Freedom of speech.

 Freedom of press.

 Freedom of assembly.

 2nd: The right to bear arms.

 3rd: Limits the quartering of soldiers.

 4th: Limits searches and seizures.

 5th: Rights of persons accused of a crime.

 6th: Right to a speedy trial.

 7th: Jury trial in civil cases.

 8th: Excessive bail or punishment forbidden.

9th: Citizens entitled to rights not listed in the Constitution.

 10th: Powers reserved to the states or people.

 11th: Rules for lawsuits against states (1798).

 12th: New way of electing the President and Vice President (1804).

 13th: Slavery abolished (1865).

 14th: Guarantees citizenship, due process, and equal protection under the law (1868).

 15th: Protects voting rights (1870).

 16th: Rights of federal government to collect income taxes (1913).

 17th: Election of senators by the people (1913).

 18th: Banned the sale of alcohol (1919).

 19th: Women given the vote (1920).

 20th: Sets date when terms of the President and Congress begin (1933).

 21st: Repeals 18th amendment (1933).

 22nd: Limits the President to two terms (1951).

 23rd: Gives people in the District of Columbia the right to vote for president (1961).

 24th: Forbids paying tax to vote (1964).

 25th: If something happens to the President, who is next in line (1967).

 26th: Sets 18 as the voting age (1971).

Separation of Powers

King George III was the ruler of England during the Revolution. The writers of the Constitution knew that they did not want a powerful king to head their government.

The men who wrote the Constitution knew they wanted a strong national government. They also knew they did not want to give too much power to one person or one group of people. So they decided that the powers of government should be divided. This idea is called separation of powers.

Here are the branches of government and their separate powers.

Article I
Legislative Branch
Congress

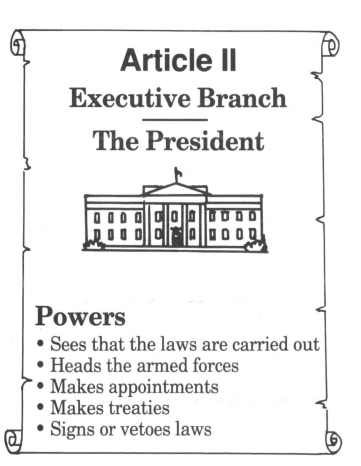

Powers
- Makes laws
- Collects taxes and borrows money
- Prints and coins money
- Provides for and maintains the armed forces

Article II
Executive Branch
The President

Powers
- Sees that the laws are carried out
- Heads the armed forces
- Makes appointments
- Makes treaties
- Signs or vetoes laws

Article III
Judicial Branch
The Supreme Court and other national courts

Powers
- Explains the meaning of laws
- Decides whether laws passed by Congress are in keeping with the Constitution

Checks and Balances

The word "check" has many meanings. One of them is to stop or limit. "Checks and balances" are the limits put on each branch of government so that one branch cannot overpower another branch.

The writers of the Constitution checked the powers they gave each branch of government. The writers also wanted all three branches to limit, or "balance," each other's powers.

President Clinton signs a bill into law.

GOVERNMENT

This mobile is a symbol of balance of power.

Here are some examples of balance of power.

Laws

 Congress passes a law, but it can't become a law unless the President gives his approval by signing it.

 The president can veto, or reject, the law. Congress can override the veto by a two-thirds vote of both the Senate and the House.

 The Supreme Court might declare the law unconstitutional.

War Powers

 The President is commander in chief of the armed forces.

 Congress has the power to declare war.

Appointments

The President can make some important appointments.

The Senate must approve the appointments.

Voting Powers

 Members of Congress and the President are elected for limited terms. If the voters want a change, they can go to the polls and vote officials out of office.

The Lawmaking Branch

The U.S. Congress meets in the Capitol Building in Washington, D.C. From this view, the Senate meets on the left side of the building and the House of Representatives meets on the right.

photo courtesy National Park Service

Article I of the Constitution

The first part, or article, of the Constitution, Article I, is about the legislative branch of the government. The men who wrote the Constitution thought that this branch was so important, they put it first. The first section of Article I says that the Constitution gives the power of making the laws to Congress. Congress is made up of two houses, the Senate and House of Representatives.

In the House

• A representative must be at least 25 years old and must have been a U.S. citizen for seven years.

• The number of representatives is based on the number of people in each state.

Today, the number of representatives is set at 435. Each representative represents about 500,000 people.

In the Senate

• A senator must be at least 30 years old and must have been a U.S. citizen for nine years.

• There are two senators from each state.

Today, there are 100 senators.

TO DO

Find Out

Who are the two senators that represent your state? Who is your district's representative? Visit your school or public library with a friend to find out this important information.

The Busy Congressional Members

Members of Congress are very busy people. They have many places to go in one day.

Here are some of the things members do:

• propose and debate, or discuss, new laws.

• meet with people from their home states to discuss their problems.

• give speeches.

• work to see that their state or district is getting treated fairly in receiving federal jobs and money.

• talk with visiting groups from their home state or district.

• attend meetings with members of their political party. (There are two main parties, the Republicans and the Democrats.)

Republican Congressman Bill Archer meets with visiting groups from his district.

Democratic Senator Carol Moseley-Braun gives a speech.

You and Article I

Congress has the power to make laws that affect your everyday life:

• the power to coin the money you spend.

• the power to set up the Postal Service that delivers your mail.

• the power to collect taxes your parents or guardians pay.

The United States Constitution

Congress was given the power to make all laws that would be "necessary and proper" for carrying out the duties given it in Article I. This has become known as the "elastic clause" because it stretches the powers of Congress to deal with many matters not in the Constitution.

Help for Members of Congress

Members of Congress couldn't get their work done without the help of their staffs.

Here are some of the jobs that members of the congressional staffs do.

Administrative Assistant: manages the Washington and district offices, runs the day-to-day operations, and often represents the member when she or he has an appointment.

Personal Appointments Secretary: handles the member's personal mail and daily schedule.

Legislative Assistant: answers mail about laws or bills, keeps track of proposals made by other members, and helps write new proposals.

Caseworker: handles voters' requests about special federal programs. Might work in either Washington or the district offices.

Receptionist: greets visitors, answers the phone, and handles requests for White House tours.

Computer Operator and File Clerk: handles mass mailings and mailing lists, opens the mail, and gets it out.

Press Secretary: answers questions from the press, writes newsletters and press releases, helps write the member's speeches, and handles news conferences.

District Office Staff: represents member of Congress while he or she is in Washington and relays voters' problems and opinions on new laws.

Pages: Congress also depends greatly on its pages. Pages are teenage boys and girls who deliver messages for members of Congress. While running errands, they learn a lot about how our government works.

Pages come to Washington from all parts of the country.

The page program is open to juniors in high school.

Senators may appoint as many as 30 pages for the Senate.

Senate pages wear blue blazers, blue pants, and white shirts. Boys wear ties.

Representatives may name as many as 66 pages for the House.

Both the House and the Senate have special schools for their pages during the school year. Their classes start as early as 6:45 in the morning! They work in the afternoon.

Pages live in a dormitory near the Capitol.

They serve from 6 months to a year.

House pages wear blue blazers, ties, gray pants or skirts, and white shirts.

TRY 'N FIND
CONGRESS

Words that remind us of Congress are hidden in the block below. See if you can find: BILL, LAW, QUORUM, CAPITOL, HILL, COMMITTEE, PROPOSED, CONGRESS, PASS, REJECT, VETO, VOTE, HOUSE, SENATE, DEBATE, MEMBERS, RULES, HEARING, ELECT, LOBBY, FLOOR, CAUCUS.

MAYBE YOU CAN VISIT YOUR CONGRESSMAN SOMEDAY!

```
R U L E S C O M M I T T E E S
X C A P I T O L C V O T E E E
Q U O R U M P Z O E P B H L N
J K C A U C U S N T A I I E A
H E A R I N G J G O S L L C T
P R O P O S E D R K S L L T E
D E B A T E S R E J E C T K P
Q U M E M B E R S X F L O O R
H O U S E L A W S L O B B Y V
```

Think About It
TO DO

Imagine you are working for one of your state's Congress members. Which job would you like to have most? Why? Share your thoughts with a friend.

Mini Spy ...

Mini Spy and Rookie are visiting a member of Congress. See if you can find: • catcher's mitt • briefcase • letter H • dustpan • drum • skirt • pineapple • word MINI • banana • frypan • cup • sausage • pocketknife • present

How a Bill Becomes a Law

The passing of a law takes paths that are very much alike in the House and Senate.

HOUSE

Here is the path a bill takes in the House before it becomes law.

1. Proposed

A bill is proposed by a representative and sent to the committee set up to handle the subject.

2. Committee Considers

Since so many bills are proposed, the committee chooses only a few for further study.

3. Hearings Held

The committee holds hearings so that interested people can say what they think about the bill. It then "marks up" (or rewrites) the bill.

4. Rules Set

Since the House has so many members, the time limit and rules for the debates are set by a special Rules Committee.

SENATE

Here is how the Senate works to pass a law.

1. Proposed

A bill is proposed by a senator and sent to the committee set up to handle the subject.

2. Committee Considers

Since so many bills are proposed, the committee chooses only a few for further study.

3. Hearings Held

The committee holds hearings so that interested people can say what they think about the bill. It then "marks up" (or rewrites) the bill.

4. Rules Set

The Senate leaders schedule the bill for debate. The Senate leaders decide the rules for debate.

The House of Representatives is made up of 435 members elected every two years from 50 states. The states are divided into districts, with an equal number of people in each one.

The Senate has 100 members, two from each state. A senator has a term for six years. One-third of the Senate is elected every two years. The terms of both senators from the same state do not end at the same time.

If a bill passes one part of Congress and is not introduced or sponsored by a senator or representative in the other one, it is sent directly to the committee handling the subject in that part. (Step 2)

5. Debates Held

The House debates or discusses the bill, changes or amends it, votes, and either passes or rejects it.

5. Debates Held

The Senate debates or discusses the bill, changes or amends it, votes, and either passes or rejects it.

6. Conference Committee Agrees

If there is a difference between the bill passed in the House and the one passed in the Senate, a conference committee works out the differences.

7. Approval

The rewritten bill is sent back for a "yes" or "no" vote by the members.

7. Approval

The rewritten bill is sent back to the Senate for a "yes" or "no" vote by the members.

8. President Signs

The bill is sent to the President for signing. If he vetoes it, the bill is sent back to the House and Senate. If it passes again with a two-thirds vote of each house, it becomes a law.

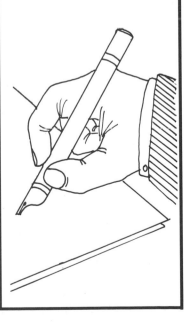

The Capitol

The U.S. Capitol in Washington, D.C., is one of the most famous buildings in the world.

It has become a powerful symbol of our government because of what goes on inside.

Our Congress meets there and passes laws that affect all of us. What our country does also affects people around the world.

This is a view from the West Front of the Capitol. Every four years our presidents take their oath of office here at the start of their terms.

The Capitol was designed in 1792 by William Thornton. The first wing of the Capitol Building was completed in 1800. Congress and the Supreme Court both met in it for more than 100 years.

As our country grew, so did the Capitol.

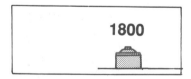

1. First wing.

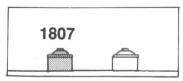

2. Second wing.

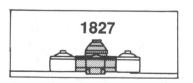

3. Middle section.

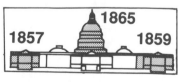

4. Bigger dome and two more wings.

My, how it has grown!

Today the Capitol is:
- 350 feet deep (about the length of a football field)
- 751 feet long (about the length of two football fields)

It has:
- 540 rooms
- 658 windows
- 850 doorways
- 180 fireplaces
- 16 1/2 acres of floor space
- grounds that cover 181 acres

14

The Capitol does not have a back and front. It has a West Front and an East Front. This is the East Front. It has a porch with a pointed roof.

photo courtesy Architect of the Capitol

1. The House Chamber has benches for the 435 members. Representatives do not usually have specially assigned seats.

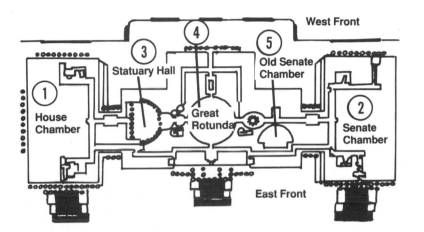

West Front

3

4

5

Statuary Hall

Old Senate Chamber

1

House Chamber

Great Rotunda

2

Senate Chamber

East Front

photo courtesy Architect of the Capitol

2. The Senate Chamber has assigned seats for its 100 senators. The Democrats sit on one side and the Republicans on the other.

photo courtesy Architect of the Capitol

3. Statuary Hall is one of the rooms where statues are displayed. Each state can send statues of two of its most outstanding citizens.

photo courtesy Architect of the Capitol

4. The Great Rotunda is a circular room in the center of the Capitol, under the dome.

Write to Them

After finding out who represents you in Congress, you might want to write to them:

Senator _____
The United States Senate
Washington, D.C. 20510
Representative _____
House of Representatives
Washington, D.C. 20515

5. The Old Senate Chamber has been restored to look like it did back in 1824. This photo shows the Vice President's desk.

photo by Betty Debnam

15

The Executive Branch

Article II of the Constitution

As you just learned, the legislative branch makes this country's laws. But it is up to the executive branch to carry out these laws. Article II of the Constitution sets up the executive branch, which is headed by our President.

The President lives and has his offices in the White House in Washington, D.C.

Section I of Article II says that the executive power shall be vested (put) in a president of the United States of America. He shall hold his office during the term of four years, together with a vice president, who is chosen for the same term.

The First Oath-Taking

Our first president, George Washington, was sworn into office on April 30, 1789.

He was supposed to take office in March, but Congress was not ready.

One of the things that held up Congress was deciding how he should be addressed. They decided on "President of the United States."

Thousands cheered as Washington took the oath on the balcony of Federal Hall in New York City.

16

The President's Job

When a new president comes into office, he must take the president's oath that appears in Article II.

The Oath:

"I do solemnly swear [or affirm] that I will faithfully execute the office of president of the United States, and will to the best of my ability, preserve, protect, and defend the Constitution of the United States."

Qualifications*

To become president, a person must:
• be at least 35 years old.
• be a native-born citizen.
• have lived in this country for 14 years.

* (kwal-uh-fuh-kay-shuns: skills and abilities needed for a job.)

Benefits

As the leader of our country, the President has a very big job. But he also is given many benefits, or advantages.

Experts say that for anyone to have the benefits that a president has, he must make about $30 million a year!

His benefits include:
• the rent-free White House (132 rooms).
• jet planes, helicopters, and a fleet of cars.
• excellent medical care.
• many chances to travel.

Inaugural Speech

Here is a famous quote from an inaugural speech.

"Ask not what your country can do for you; ask what you can do for your country."
—John F. Kennedy, Jan. 20, 1961

★ ★ ★ ★ ★ ★ ★

George Washington gave the shortest inauguration speech ever, 133 words, at his second inauguration in 1793.

Term | 1993 | 1994 | 1995 | 1996 |

A president can serve two terms (periods of time) of four years each, or eight years total. He can serve up to 10 years if he takes over the unfinished term of another president.

Find Out

Do you know which President was in office the year you were born? Look in an almanac or an encyclopedia to find out who the President was at the time of your birth. List some facts you find out about him.

The President's Many Hats

I AM READING ABOUT HIS PLAN TO CREATE MORE JOBS.

COMMANDER IN CHIEF

As commander in chief, the President is in charge of our armed forces. He must see that they are ready for combat.

The President doesn't really wear these hats, but this expression is a way of saying that he has a job with many duties.

Cut out President Clinton and the hats he might wear:
  Make a president's jobs display.
  Watch the newspaper. Put the hat on him that fits the job in the story.

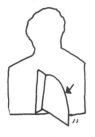

Trace around the President's picture on a piece of cardboard. Glue the photo to the cardboard.

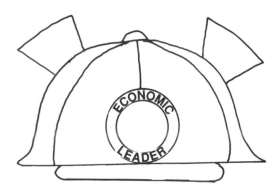

ECONOMIC LEADER

As economic leader, the President has to try to keep prices from going up and up. He must also try to keep our businesses busy and our workers on the job.

PARTY LEADER

CUT HERE ↑

President Bill Clinton, First Lady Hillary Clinton, Vice President Al Gore and his wife, Tipper. This photo was taken during the campaign. To show the role they were playing, they would be wearing Democratic Party hats.

As party leader, the President has much influence over the way his political party thinks about national problems. He also makes speeches and tries to raise money for his party.

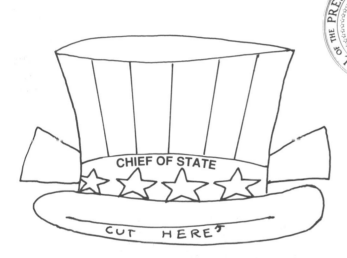

CHIEF OF STATE

CUT HERE ↑

CHIEF DIPLOMAT

CUT HERE ↑

As chief of state, the President represents our country here and in other lands. He attends many ceremonies as a representative and symbol of the United States. A king might carry out these duties in other countries.

As chief diplomat, the President helps decide how our country will act toward other countries. He picks the ambassadors (people who represent the President in other countries), whom the Senate approves.

As chief executive, the President is the boss of millions of U.S. government employees. He also must propose laws to Congress that he thinks should be passed.

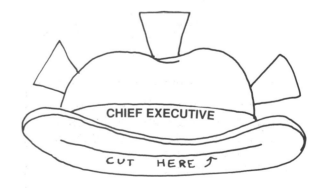

CHIEF EXECUTIVE

CUT HERE ↑

19

The President's Cabinet

Do you have some friends whom you turn to for advice? The President of the United States does. He has a Cabinet.

Members of the Cabinet head up big departments. Most are called secretaries. The number of Cabinet members changes as our country's needs change.

A president nominates his own Cabinet members, but his choices must be approved by the Senate. Here are the 14 different positions in the Cabinet:

1. Secretary of State
Works out agreements with other countries.

2. Secretary of the Treasury
Supervises the collection of taxes and the printing of money.

3. Secretary of Defense
Is in charge of the armed forces.

4. The Attorney General
Enforces the U.S. government's laws.

5. Secretary of the Interior
Protects natural resources and wildlife.

6. Secretary of Agriculture
Looks over the needs of farmers.

7. Secretary of Commerce
Is interested in better U.S. business opportunities here and in other countries.

8. Secretary of Labor
Looks after the interests of U.S. workers.

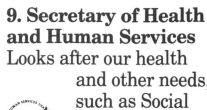

9. Secretary of Health and Human Services
Looks after our health and other needs, such as Social Security benefits.

10. Secretary of Housing and Urban Development
Is concerned with problems of housing and city living.

11. Secretary of Transportation
Tries to set up better and safer ways to travel.

12. Secretary of Energy
Tries to solve our energy problems.

13. Secretary of Education
Tries to improve and gather information about education.

14. Secretary of Veteran Affairs
Is concerned with benefits for veterans and their families.

 **Think About It**

Can you think of some problems your community might be facing? Which members of the President's Cabinet would you talk to in order to take care of those problems?

The White House

The President lives and works in the country's most famous house, the White House.

Built in Washington, D.C., almost 200 years ago, the White House has been home to all but our first president, George Washington. But it was Washington who insisted that the White House be made of stone. He wanted it to stand for ages, just as he wanted this country to stand for ages.

To find out more about the White House, let's see what it might be like to live there.

Your Address would be:

(Write your name here)
1600 Pennsylvania Avenue
Washington, DC 20550

The North Entrance would be where you might receive visitors. It has a portico, or front porch. It faces Pennsylvania Avenue.

The South Entrance overlooks your backyard. It has a double-deck porch.

The White House is a busy place. If you were president, you would use it to:

Live in

You and your family would live on the second and third floors.

Work in

The Oval Office is in the West Wing, a section that has been added on.

Hold meetings in

You would hold many important meetings inside and outside. On a pretty day, you might have a ceremony in the Rose Garden outside your office.

When the original White House was built, it had 36 rooms. By adding two basement floors and a top floor, it now has 132 rooms within the same walls. It has:
- six floors, including two basements
- 34 bathrooms
- 11 bedrooms

The East and West wings were added later.

Your house would be a very unusual place. The White House is the only home of a head of state that is open on a regular basis to visitors free of charge.

Visitors see rooms only on the first and ground floors.

The First Floor plan

WEST WING (Executive Offices)

Oval Office

Rose Garden

State Dining Room

Red Room

Blue Room

Green Room

Entrance Hall

Cross Hall

East Room

South Porch

Jacqueline Kennedy Garden

EAST WING (Public tours start here)

You would use the:
State Dining Room for seating 140 people; Red, Green, Blue Rooms for small gatherings; East Room for bigger meetings and entertaining.

State Dining Room

Red Room

Blue Room

Green Room

East Room

You usually would not see the visitors nor would they see you.

TO DO

Map It
What does your home look like? Do certain rooms have special purposes? Draw and label a map of your house.

The Judicial Branch

The Supreme Court meets in this building in Washington, D.C. During its history it has met in several different places. The words "Equal Justice Under Law" are carved above the columns.

From the collection of the Supreme Court of the United States.

Our Court Systems

There are two main systems of courts in the United States.

State courts get their power from state constitutions and laws.

Federal, or U.S., courts, get their power from the U.S. Constitution and laws of Congress.

In both state and federal court systems, there are:

Trial courts: where the facts or evidence are presented and a decision is made by a judge or a jury. Most cases start here. This is called a lower court.

Courts of appeal: where judges review what went on in a trial court and decide if the trial was conducted in a way that was fair and according to the law.

The Right of Appeal

Any person or group can appeal their case to the U.S. Supreme Court.

In one recent year, 6,300 cases were appealed.

Of that number, the Court ruled on 125 cases.

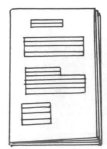

Lawyers put their petition, or written request for a hearing, in a booklet that must be a certain size.

People who cannot afford lawyers might handwrite their appeals.

Article III

Article III of the Constitution establishes the judicial branch (or court system) of the U.S. government.

The first section of Article III says that the judicial power (the power of the courts) shall be vested (put) in one Supreme Court and such inferior (lower) courts as Congress might establish.

Role of the Supreme Court

- Explain the meaning of laws
- Decide if laws are constitutional or not

The Supreme Court

The most important court, and the last court that a person or a group can appeal to, is the U.S. Supreme Court.

It has the power to review decisions made by both federal and state courts.

Its main job is to decide if a lower court decision is in keeping with the rules set down by the U.S. Constitution.

It can also decide if a law passed by Congress is constitutional or not.

Once it rules in a case, its decisions must be obeyed, or followed, by local, state, and federal courts.

Its decisions affect the lives of millions of Americans.

The Supreme Court justices in 1987.

The Bill of Rights

Many of the decisions the Supreme Court has made in the past years have been based on the Bill of Rights and the 14th Amendment.

The amendments limit the power of government.

Justices

It is a great honor to be a member of the Supreme Court. Members are appointed by the President, but must be approved by the Senate.

The nine judges are called justices. There are eight associate justices and one chief justice.

They are appointed for life or until they resign.

This prevents a president from removing justices from their job if he does not like the decisions they make.

The Court at Work

The justices usually select the cases they will hear. They choose very important ones that have strong arguments on both sides.

The justices study the records of each case they agree to hear. They read "briefs," or written arguments, sent in by lawyers. Each justice has four clerks, young lawyers who do research on the cases under consideration.

The justices hold hearings to listen to oral, or spoken, arguments presented by lawyers on each side.

Each side has 30 minutes to present its case. The justices also ask questions during this time. The public and press can attend these hearings in the courtroom.

The Justices at Work

Secrecy

The justices hold conferences to discuss the cases.

No one but the nine justices can be in the room. The newest member to the court serves as doorkeeper.

What goes on in these meetings is top secret so the justices can freely discuss each case.

The Decisions

The justices base their decisions on:
- **the U.S. Constitution**
- **laws passed by Congress**
- **other rulings they have made in the past.**

When at least five of the justices agree, one justice usually writes the majority opinion on the decision.

The decision is announced in court, handed out to the press, and put into the records.

Then the decision is the law of the land.

Courtesy and Respect

Before the conferences and before each court session, each justice shakes hands with the other eight. This tradition started years ago to remind the judges that they can remain friends although they might disagree.

The U.S. Supreme Court is a very dignified place.

The court gets its power from the Constitution and the respect that the people have for it and its decisions.

Judicial Review

From the collection of the Supreme Court of the United States.

Chief Justice John Marshall (1755-1835) helped establish judicial review.

Judicial review is one of the most powerful traditions of the Supreme Court. This tradition allows the court to review laws and decide if they are in keeping with the Constitution. Judicial review is not mentioned in the Constitution but it has been in use since the case of *Marbury vs. Madison* was decided in 1803.

In this famous case, the Supreme Court ruled that a law passed by Congress was not constitutional. The opinion in *Marbury vs. Madison* was written by Chief Justice John Marshall.

TO DO **Think About It**

Knowing that there are nine justices of the Supreme Court, can you guess why a decision passes after at least five members agree?

The Chief Justices of the United States

The chief justices do not change much. Since the first Chief Justice
took office, we have had only 16 chief justices.
During that same period, we have had 42 presidents.

1. John Jay,
New York
(1789-1795)

2. John Rutledge,
South Carolina
(1795)

3. Oliver Ellsworth,
Connecticut
(1796-1800)

4. John Marshall,
Virginia
(1801-1835)

5. Roger B.
Taney, Maryland
(1836-1864)

6. Salmon P. Chase,
New Hampshire
(1864-1873)

7. Morrison R. Waite,
Connecticut
(1874-1888)

8. Melville W. Fuller,
Maine
(1888-1910)

9. Edward D. White,
Louisiana
(1910-1921)

10. William H. Taft,
Ohio
(1921-1930)

11. Charles E. Hughes,
New York
(1930-1941)

12. Harlan F. Stone,
New Hampshire
(1941-1946)

13. Fred M. Vinson,
Kentucky
(1946-1953)

14. Earl Warren,
California
(1953-1969)

15. Warren E. Burger,
Minnesota
(1969-1986)

16. William H. Rehnquist,
Wisconsin
(1986-   )

The Supreme Court Building

Completed in 1935, The Supreme Court building was designed to look like a Greek temple.

On the left side of the main steps is a seated marble figure, the Contemplation of Justice.

The Supreme Court faces the United States Capitol. It has marble columns that sit atop 36 steps rising from a huge white plaza. Above these marble columns are the words "Equal Justice Under Law."

The main floor is largely occupied by the justices' chambers, offices for law clerks and secretaries, and the large formal East and West conference rooms.

On the right side of the steps is another marble figure, the Guardian, or Authority, of Law.

The Supreme Court Term

The hearings are held in a beautiful courtroom. The justices sit in a row on a raised platform.

The Supreme Court's "term," or year, starts the first Monday in October.

Each term is divided into "sittings" and recesses.

For two weeks, the court "sits," or hears the cases. For the next two weeks it is in recess. During this time, the justices write their decisions.

The justices carefully study the records for each case that comes before them. They read the "briefs," or written arguments, sent in by lawyers.

The justices ask the lawyers questions while they are appearing before the court. Each side has 30 minutes to present its case.

During the summer months when the court is not in session, the justices work to decide what cases they will consider the next term.

The court is asked to rule on thousands of cases each year. Generally the justices agree to hear only about 150 cases.

Think About It

What do the words "Equal Justice Under Law" mean to you? Explain the meaning of the words in a brief paragraph that includes examples of "equal justice."

Let's Visit the National Archives
Keeping the Constitution Safe

The Building

National Archives photos

Because the Constitution is the foundation for how the U. S. government works, it is one of our most valued treasures. The original document is kept in the National Archives. Archives are places where records are stored. The building has 72 columns and the largest brass doors in the world.

The Exhibit Hall

The Constitution is displayed in a big marble exhibit hall shaped like a half-circle. Marble steps lead up to the display case. A huge painting hangs on either side. Visitors are quiet when they enter the darkened hall. They are not allowed to take flash photographs.

The Pages

The first page of the Constitution begins with the words "We the People." There are four pages. Pages 1 through 4 contain the preamble and text. The signatures are on page 4. There is also a fifth page. It is a resolution from the convention sending the Constitution to the Congress.

The Display Cases

Information about the Declaration of Independence and the Constitution

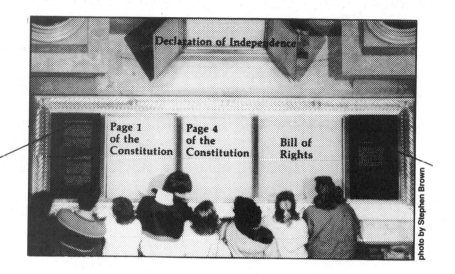

Page 1 of the Constitution

Page 4 of the Constitution

Bill of Rights

Information about the Bill of Rights

photo by Stephen Brown

Two pages of the Constitution, 1 and 4, are usually displayed in cases alongside the Bill of Rights. The Declaration of Independence hangs above. The pages are of parchment, or animal skin. They are in separate airtight cases filled with helium gas. Special protective glass helps keep them from fading.

The Vault

Every night and in emergencies, the cases are lowered to a 55-ton concrete and steel vault 22 feet below the display. The mechanical jack that raises and lowers the cases is operated by electricity with backup batteries.

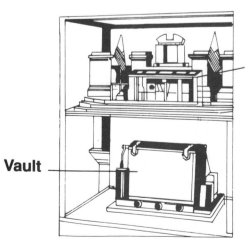

Display cases

Vault

BASSET BROWN THE NEWS HOUND'S

TRY 'N FIND

NATIONAL ARCHIVES

Words that remind us of the National Archive are hidden in the block below. See if you can find: EXHIBITION HALL, QUILL, ARCHIVES, PRESERVATION, WASHINGTON, HELIUM, INK, PAGES, FOUR, DOCUMENT, AMERICA, ANNIVERSARY, BICENTENNIAL, SIGNERS.

DO YOU HAVE A COPY OF THE CONSTITUTION?

WE THE PEOPLE

```
E X H I B I T I O N H A L L D
B A P A N N I V E R S A R Y O
C M A B C Y S I G N E R S S C
L E G A R C H I V E S O F Q U
P R E S E R V A T I O N O U M
I I S W H E L I U M T O U I E
N C W A S H I N G T O N R L N
K A B I C E N T E N N I A L T
```

Newspaper Readers Learn About the U.S. Government

Everytown, Today — By reading news stories about the President, members of Congress, and Supreme Court justices, newspaper readers become informed citizens.

photo by Christina Craver

Families have fun reading newspapers and learning together.

FRONT PAGE NEWS

Keep up with the latest events in Washington, D.C. Look through your newspaper for news about our national government. Which branches of government is it about? Talk about the article with a friend.

CLASSIFIED ADS

Pretend you are a member of Congress looking for a congressional page. Write a help-wanted ad with a job description.

HOT OFF THE PRESS

Pretend you are a newspaper reporter and you are about to interview a very important person in Washington, D.C.

Decide whom to interview— the President, a member of Congress, or a Supreme Court justice. Make a list of questions to ask. Then have a partner play the role of the interviewee to answer all your questions. Then write a news story. Let your friends discover just how much you know about the U.S. government!

Reporters on the Job

Congress members, the President, and the Supreme Court justices aren't the only ones who work in Washington, D.C. Newspaper reporters spend a lot of time there, too. Their work is to keep people across the country up to date on the latest events.

Who wrote about the government in today's paper? Look at the by-lines to find out.

More Government News

Reporters don't just write about the U.S. government. Look through your local newspaper to see what's happening in your state and local government, too.